Catherine Veitch · Shiori Saito

MEET THE
NATIONAL
ANIMALS

Fun animal facts from around the world

In memory of extinct animals and in celebration
of the animals we have. Let's treasure them. C.V.

To our animal friends around the world
who we should admire and protect. S.S.

The Quarto Group
Inspiring | Educating | Creating | Entertaining

Brimming with creative inspiration, how-to projects, and useful information to enrich your everyday life, quarto.com is a favorite destination for those pursuing their interests and passions.

Author: Catherine Veitch
Illustrator: Shiori Saito
Designer: Sarah Chapman-Suire
Commissioning Editor: Carly Madden
Creative Director: Malena Stojić
Associate Publisher: Rhiannon Findlay

© 2022 Quarto Publishing plc
Illustration © 2022 Shiori Saito

Shiori Saito has asserted her right to be identified as the illustrator of this work.

First published in 2021 by Happy Yak, an imprint of The Quarto Group.
26391 Crown Valley Parkway, Suite 220, Mission Viejo, CA 92691, USA.
T: +1 949 380 7510 F: +1 949 380 7575 **www.quarto.com**

A CIP record for this book is available from the Library of Congress.

ISBN 978 0 7112 7445 7

Manufactured in Guangdong, China TT062022

9 8 7 6 5 4 3 2

MIX
Paper from
responsible sources
FSC
www.fsc.org   FSC® C016973

CONTENTS

Wild about animals

Many beautiful animals roam our planet... with fabulous fur and fast feet, terrific teeth and twitching tails, even curly claws and shiny scales. Did you know that countries have their own national animals? A country may choose an animal that lives there or it may be because it's strong or helpful.

Brown Bear is the national animal of Finland. One day he decided that it would be a grr-eat idea to gather up some other national animals to celebrate their grr-eatness. Follow Brown Bear's journey along the bottom of the pages and see which animals he can find. Along the way spot amazing flags from different countries and discover why some animals were chosen as national animals, things that make the animals special, and even some of their naughty habits, which have nothing to do with the countries they live in.

Brown bear

I have a thick warm coat to help me survive the freezing winters in Finland. While I have fun in the snow, my mate and her cubs are warm and toasty in their den, and hibernating for the whole winter!

Follow me as I meet new friends. Look at the picture strip at the bottom of each page.

FINLAND

This bear can sleep through anything. She didn't even wake up when she gave birth!

Zzzz

Polar bear

The brown bear is super tough, but I'm the biggest bear in the world. I'm the national animal of icy Greenland.

My nose never lets me down and I can smell when a pesky seal is under the ice. I'll wait all day for it if I have to—it won't outsmart me!

Super-sized paw, as big as a dinner plate!

GREENLAND

Seal's breathing hole

Dromedary camel

I'm super helpful and have carried people and their things across this hot, sandy desert long before cars came along. I'm not surprised Kuwait chose me as its national animal.

KUWAIT

This is a beast of a sandstorm! Lucky for me, I can close my nostrils to keep out the dusty sand... and any other intruders!

Llama

Hello, I'm on the flag of Bolivia. I'm just as helpful as the camel and a whiz at walking up steep, rocky mountain slopes.

It gets chilly the higher up you go. But my soft wool saves the day as it makes lovely warm clothes.

BOLIVIA

Bald eagle

I was chosen as the national animal of the United States of America because of my good looks, strength, and long life!

I make my nest high up on towering mountains, where you will see me gliding magnificently over the mountaintops.

UNITED STATES OF AMERICA

Flamingo

You'll find me in salty lagoons in the sunny Bahamas, often with my head upside-down in squelchy mud searching for shrimps. I can't eat enough of them! In fact, I eat so many that they turn my feathers bright pink.

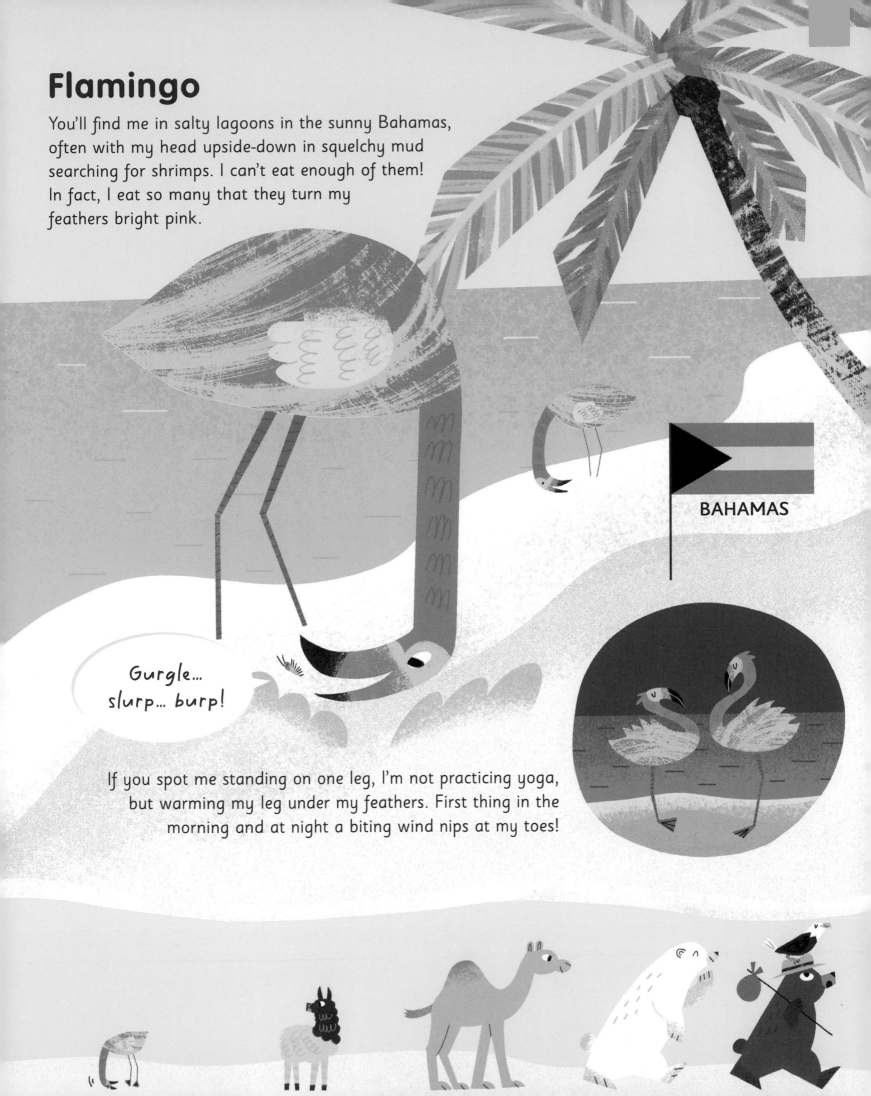

BAHAMAS

Gurgle... slurp... burp!

If you spot me standing on one leg, I'm not practicing yoga, but warming my leg under my feathers. First thing in the morning and at night a biting wind nips at my toes!

Tiger

India is proud to have me as its national animal as I'm strong and super-fit. I have over 100 stripes, which help to camouflage me when I'm hunting in the thick mangrove forest where I live. Perfect for hide-and-seek!

Just as every human has a different fingerprint, every tiger has a different pattern of stripes.

INDIA

Black panther

I'm just as good at hide-and-seek! I'm the national animal of Gabon, and my nickname is the ghost of the forest because I'm so good at hiding and keeping quiet when I hunt. Few humans have seen me.

I can make myself heard when I want to, and can roar, hiss, growl, and even scream!

GABON

Fennec fox

Don't be fooled by my cute looks as I am a fearsome fox who survives in the sweltering hot desert of Algeria.

I even have a football team named after me.

Go, The Fennecs!

ALGERIA

I snooze in my burrow during the day. Even the juiciest locust won't tempt me outside in this heat!

Sand cat

I'm no cuddly kitty either, as I too live in a boiling desert, but in Uzbekistan. No cans of cat food for me. I hunt mice, birds, spiders, insects, and even snakes for my dinner! I can even bark like a dog!

Markhor

Look at my magnificent horns! They grow up to 63 inches (160 cm) long—that's taller than you! In Pakistan, where I live, my name means *snake eater* because my horns look like curled snakes and people thought I actually ate snakes. But I have better manners than that, and plants are more to my taste.

← Daring mountaineer!

Male

Female

My stylish split hooves grip onto rocks and I can zip up the mountains to escape from hungry wolves.

PAKISTAN

Oryx

My sleek horns are just as splendid. If I turn sideways, it looks like I have only one horn—I could pass for a unicorn, don't you think?

UNITED ARAB EMIRATES

I'm made for living in the hot desert, in the United Arab Emirates. My white coat keeps me cool in the burning sun, and thanks to my wide hooves it's easy-peasy to walk over the sand without sinking.

Giant panda

I'm special in China because I don't live wild anywhere else in the world. My species has been around for over two million years, and we're so well-loved we're no longer endangered. Amazing!

CHINA

I'm a peaceful panda, perfectly happy just eating bamboo and sleeping. I can munch bamboo for up to 14 hours a day! All that chomping gives my jaw a workout and makes it superhero-strong. Excuse me now, as I need to sleep... zzzzz.

Red kangaroo

That rare bear really is special. Although, people come from all over the world to Australia just to see me. But there are a lot more of me! There are over 50 million of us in Australia—that's more kangaroos than people!

AUSTRALIA

Hold on tight... it's going to be a bumpy ride!

There are so many of us roos that you'll even see our picture on road signs warning drivers to watch out for us crossing the road.

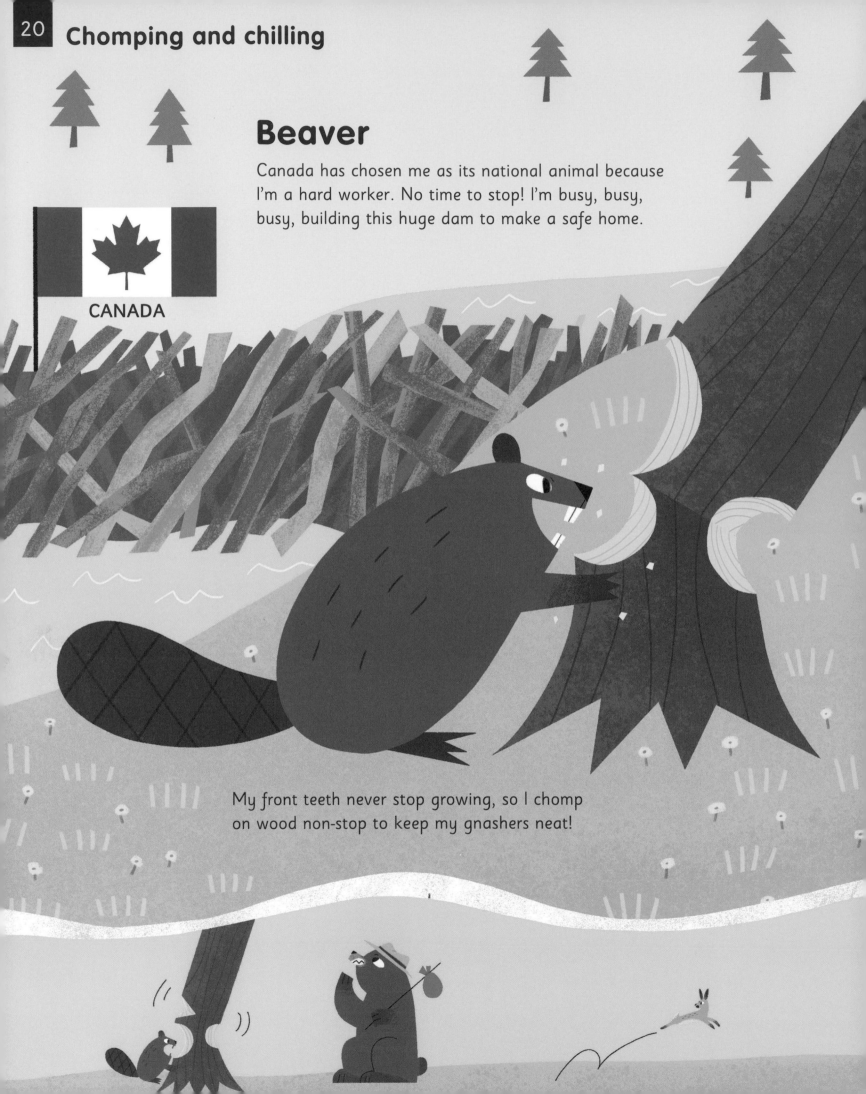

Beaver

Canada has chosen me as its national animal because I'm a hard worker. No time to stop! I'm busy, busy, busy, building this huge dam to make a safe home.

CANADA

My front teeth never stop growing, so I chomp on wood non-stop to keep my gnashers neat!

Mountain hare

That beaver needs to chill! I just flatten plants and snuggle down in a hollow to make a comfy home, here in this green country of Ireland. Sometimes I try my luck and move into an empty rabbit's burrow!

IRELAND

NO ENTRY!

Wow!

Don't ever call me a rabbit, though. I'm a hare and, in my humble opinion, much more handsome than a rabbit, with longer back legs and ears!

Gallic rooster

A long time ago I was chosen as the national animal of France... but it was entirely by accident! When the Romans arrived in France, they called the local people Gauls. Their word for Gaul also means rooster! What a to-doodle-do!

The French were stuck with me, but, luckily, I grew on them. Soon I appeared on stamps, coins, and sports uniforms.

FRANCE

Raggiana bird-of-paradise

The people on the leafy island of Papua New Guinea are so proud to have me as their national animal that they put me on their flag.

(Unimpressed) female

I like to show off and will jump at the chance to shimmy and shake my colorful feathers to attract a mate.

(Flamboyant) males

Kwee, kwee! Check out my feathers!

Kwa, kwa! I'm the most handsome bird in this forest.

PAPUA NEW GUINEA

Mythical dragon

Legends tell of dragons from long ago in the green hills and valleys of Wales. They tell how kings would march into battle carrying pictures of dragons. The kings wanted to show how strong they were. Nothing beats a fire-breathing beast!

Most helpful guest at a BBQ!

WALES

The Welsh rugby team is even nicknamed the Dragons!

Komodo dragon

When it comes to dragons, I'm the real deal. I live in the steamy forests of Indonesia and was chosen as the national animal because you'll not find me living wild anywhere else in the world.

INDONESIA

Super-sniffer tongue to smell prey

Okay, I don't breathe actual fire, but some clever young komodos cover themselves in poop to hide their smell from other animals that want to eat them.

Protective poop activated!

Grey wolf

Italy chose me as its national animal because I am a hero in one of its legends. In the story I play a brave wolf who saves twin brothers Romulus and Remus, who were left to die as babies.

I took care of the brothers, who became famous years later when they founded the city of Rome.

Crocodile

Crocodiles like me are special on the island of Timor-Leste, where local people call us their grandfathers because some believe that they are descended from us.

People tell stories of a crocodile who lived here a long time ago and made friends with a human boy. When it was time for the legendary crocodile to die, it turned itself into this island.

TIMOR-LESTE

The mountains look just like the scaly bumps on my back!

Lion

I'm the national animal of England but I don't live in the wild here. I was chosen hundreds of years ago when King Richard I marched with paintings of me to show he was as brave and strong as I am.

The English football team is nicknamed The Three Lions.

ENGLAND

Leopard

I'm the national animal of Rwanda and you'll find me in its mountains, rainforests, and grassy plains. I'm super springy and can leap 20 feet—that's as long as three people! I need a rest after all that bouncing!

GIBRALTAR

Barbary macaque

You'll see lots of us climbing over the huge limestone Rock of Gibraltar. I can be cheeky when I try to steal your food, but please don't feed me as your snacks are not good for me. Leaves, roots, and fruit like these acorns are my all-time favorite bites to eat.

And now, for my superpower... I can stuff my super-stretchy cheeks with lots and lots of food to eat later! Don't want to get "hangry"!

Ring-tailed lemur

Like those cheeky monkeys, I can also be mischievous... especially when taking part in a stink fight over a mate! I cover my tail in smelly scent and dangle it in the face of a rival lemur to shoo it away. Stink-a-licious!

MADAGASCAR

I was chosen as the national animal of Madagascar as this island is the only place I live in the wild. Excuse me while I relax in the sunshine with my friends and warm up. I like a warm belly!

Manx cat

Hundreds of years ago, cats like me were born on the Isle of Man *without* tails. Today many cats here don't have a tail.

Since I became the island's national animal I've become a bit of a celebrity. People love coming to see me.

ISLE OF MAN

No pictures, please!

Tornjak

When I'm not busy herding sheep in the countryside of Bosnia and Herzegovina, I can be a lovable pet, too.

BOSNIA AND HERZEGOVINA

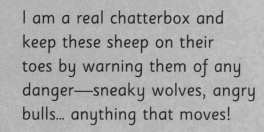

I am a real chatterbox and keep these sheep on their toes by warning them of any danger—sneaky wolves, angry bulls... anything that moves!

Common dolphin

I live in the sparkling blue seas swirling around the islands of Greece. Greek people have grown up with stories of heroic dolphins like me saving peeople's lives, so they made me their national animal.

I never sleep! Instead, I rest one side of my brain at a time. You can tell I'm resting as one eye is closed!

I have my eye on her!

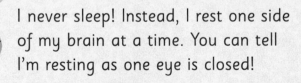

GREECE

Hawksbill turtle

That dolphin has most certainly been around for a long time, but I've lived on this planet longer than people!

SOLOMON ISLANDS

You'll find me in the warm seas around the Solomon Islands. I live among the colorful coral reef, which is bursting with life. I get my strange name from my pointy beak, which looks like the bill of a hawk.

Handy tool for pulling out tasty sponges.

Nom, nom, nom.

Andean condor

For hundreds of years, people in Colombia have written stories about me, and admired my power and long life. Look at me soar thousands of feet above the spectacular Andes Mountains—I'm much higher than even the tallest building in the world!

Oooh look! Teeny, tiny llamas!

I'll let you into the secret of how a heavy bird like me can fly so high—I float on the wind. Shh, don't tell the other animals!

COLOMBIA

Giraffe

Well, I'm the tallest animal on land! I can see all around from up here. People in Tanzania chose me for their national animal because I remind them to look at things in different ways.

TANZANIA

Unicorn

If I'm make-believe (that's up to you to decide), how did I become the national animal of Scotland? It began long ago when Scottish kings marched with pictures of unicorns to show they were brave and powerful, just like me. And I've had the job ever since!

SCOTLAND

There are many stories about my bravery and superpowers. One story describes how I dipped my magical horn into water poisoned by a sneaky snake and made it safe to drink again.

Okapi

Well, I'm definitely real! But not many people have seen me and some don't believe I exist! I'm very shy and hide in thick, wet, green forests in the Democratic Republic of Congo. I'm only found in this forest, so it's not surprising I'm the national animal here.

I can get at tasty leaves that other animals can't reach, and strip them off the trees in no time with my extra-bendy, 12-inch (30 cm) long tongue...

... which is handy for cleaning one's ears!

DEMOCRATIC
REPUBLIC OF
CONGO

European bison

Sadly I have been hunted for hundreds of years and much of my forest home in Poland has been destroyed. People began to protect my home and helped my numbers to grow, but I am still in danger.

POLAND

I'm big and strong and can eat up to 70 pounds (32 kg) of grass and other plants a day. That makes, ahem, a lot of poop!

Black rhinoceros

There are not many of us left either as people hunt us for our horns.
I was made the national animal of Lesotho to protect our species.

I'm not really black like my name, but more brown or grey. These flies are making me itch. Thank goodness these little birds like to eat flies and peck them off me!

LESOTHO

Aaah, that's the spot!

Kiwi

I'm a bird, but I can't fly! My feathers are more like fur and I don't have a tail. Also, I have nostrils at the end of my beak. So why was a strange bird like me picked to be the national animal of New Zealand?

Well, I'm special, of course! I live only in New Zealand.

NEW ZEALAND

Snuffle, snuffle! Where are those worms?

Aldabra giant tortoise

I'm one hundred and fifty years old and one of the oldest animals on this planet! In the past, tortoises like me were hunted, but I survived on this island because it is surrounded by razor-sharp coral rock. The rocks—and the sharks—stopped people landing their boats here. You'll only find me on Aldabra Island in the Seychelles.

SEYCHELLES

Shhh... Grandma is sleeping.

Hmmm, I feel a long story coming on. Best have a power nap first. Zzzzz...

Where has Dodo gone?

Are you listening, my friends?

Good to see you all! Now, the dodo's story began around 500 years ago. Before then the dodo lived happily on this island paradise of Mauritius, enjoying life in leafy, green forests, on soft sandy beaches, and under clear blue skies.

The dodo was safe, as no animals on the island wanted to eat it.

I don't have any worries in the world.

But that all changed when explorers arrived on the island. The strange-looking dodo was a stubby bird that could not fly. And because the dodo had never seen people before, it was very friendly and trusting. The explorers easily caught it for their dinner.

Rats and monkeys from the explorers' ships scrambled ashore and gobbled the dodos' eggs.

The poor dodo didn't stand a chance and soon there were no dodos left on Mauritius.

I was made the national animal of Mauritius so my story would be remembered.

Let's celebrate!

Brown Bear and the animals were sad
to hear that Dodo was no longer around.
But Brown Bear had promised them a
party, and bears always keep their promises!

Let's celebrate each
other and the wonderful
countries we live in.

Dodo's story will remind us to look after each other and our planet.

Brown bear's brain buster

Can you remember the names of the animals and the countries they represent?

Check back to see if you were right!